Get Real

Girl Talk Teen Devotional
Real Talk with the Real God

By Patrice Brown

Cover Design: Patrice Brown
Editor: NJ Kingdom Enterprises
www.njkingdomenterprises.com

This devotional is dedicated to my daughters and all the teen girls that I have been given the opportunity to pour into. Some are now mothers and some are currently pursuing their education.

I want you to know that I heard you, but better yet, God hears you.

I pray that you all will continue to hold on to God's Unchanging Hand. I pray that the Lord continues to put people in your life that will encourage you to walk in the purpose that God has destined for you. I thank you for teaching me and allowing me to pour into you.

Love you all.

Acknowledgment

I acknowledge my mother who had to deal with me as a teen.

I also have to acknowledge the Lord, Jesus Christ, who poured this work into me in a matter of hours.

I need to acknowledge Enhance Your Chance (EYC) nonprofit organization, which planted the seed for this by allowing me to work in the gift that God has given me and move in my purpose of being able to pour into young ladies.

TABLE OF CONTENTS

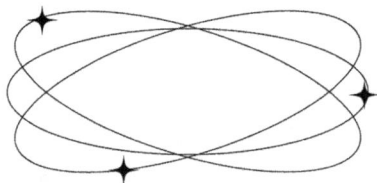

Introduction

Have you ever felt like you're lost in a sea of emotions, wondering if anyone truly understands what you're going through? Do you find yourself grappling with feelings of loneliness, doubt, or envy, and wishing for a space where you can sort through it all? If you're nodding your head, you're not alone. This devotional is here to walk alongside you on a journey of self-discovery and spiritual growth, especially designed for girls just like you. Imagine a safe place where you can explore your thoughts and feelings, journal your struggles and victories, and connect deeply with your faith.

Each chapter is crafted to be more than just a reading experience; it's your chance to reflect and engage directly with the challenges you face every day. You'll find heartfelt prayers and biblical insights that shine light on those heavy feelings, helping you to navigate through them with grace.

As you dive into themes of self-worth, the importance of friendships, and the beauty of gratitude, you'll be prompted to pause and think about how these messages resonate in your life. You'll even have the opportunity to express your feelings in dedicated journaling spaces, creating a personal record of your journey towards healing and strength.

Through this devotional, you may discover that every challenge is an opportunity for growth and that you're never truly alone. With encouragement and guided reflections, you'll come away not just with deeper insights, but with a stronger, more personal relationship with God. So grab your favorite pen and get ready to embark on a transformative journey of faith, self-exploration, and renewal—all while knowing that God's light has always been with you. Let's explore this sacred path together!

I'm Not Worthy...

"For we are his workmanship [His own master work, a work of art], created in Christ Jesus reborn from above-spiritually transformed, renewed, ready to be used for good works, which God prepared [for us] beforehand, so that we would walk in them [living the good life which he prearranged and made ready for us]." - Ephesians 2:10

Who am I? I look at other people and they seem to always have the best life. They have the newest shoes. They have the cutest clothes. They have the most updated phone. Some of them are always getting acknowledged for the things they do. Teachers are always laughing and joking with them. I'm hidden in the background. When they're around, no one notices me.

When people do notice me, I wish they wouldn't. They point at me. I feel like they're always whispering about me. They look at me from the corner of their eyes. They always seem to be sizing me up. Their faces are always frowned up.

I just feel like I'm worthless. Why am I even here? I'm just taking up space.

Prayer: Lord, show me who I am through You and in Your eyesight. No longer will I view myself as unworthy. No longer will I allow my thoughts to be contrary to Your Word. Lord, strengthen me so that I believe that Your Word is true. I am Your masterpiece. I am Your creation. You are the King of Kings and Lord of Lords. That makes me royalty.

Take a moment to capture your thoughts, feelings and responses to what you just read.

_____

_____

_____

_____

_____

_____

_____

_____

_____

_____

_____

_____

_____

_____

_____

_____

_____

_____

But I Feel Alone...

"Be strong and courageous, do not be afraid or tremble [in dread] Before them, for it is the Lord your God who goes with you. He will not fail you or abandon you."
- Deuteronomy 31:16

Sometimes, I feel there is no one I can turn to. I have so much on my mind, but I don't know who I can trust. As a result of past experiences, I am afraid to be vulnerable, so I feel alone. Even in a room filled with people, I feel alone. I smile, I joke around, I may look like I am part of the "in-crowd;" I even have a group of friends that I walk around with; but at the same time, I feel alone.

If only someone knew what I was going through. If there was only someone that I could trust with my innermost feelings and thoughts. If there was only someone who would not judge me, make fun of me, or tell my business to everybody. If there was someone around that would just listen to me and value what I have to say. If there was someone around that could give me advice. If there was someone around that would just comfort me and keep me in some type of peace. Even though there are a ton of people around, I still feel alone.

There is someone. The Lord says: "He is always with me." The Lord says: "I can trust Him." The Lord says: "He will never abandon me. He will not fail me."

But how do I do it? How do I continue to seek Him and continue to confide in Him?

"The Lord is near to the brokenhearted and saves those who are crushed in spirit (contrite in heart, truly sorry for their sin)." Psalm 34:18

Prayer: Lord, when I feel alone, remind me that You are always with me. Teach me how to build a relationship with You. Teach me how to be vulnerable and open with You. Teach me how to grow my faith and trust in You. Begin to bring people in my life that are from You, God. Plant those around me that are aligned with my purpose and will not lead me astray from You. Lord help me, take time to increase my prayer life and increase my relationship with You. Increase my faith. Help me in the places of my unbelief.

Let me believe without any doubt: You are always with me. I am never alone.

Take a moment to capture your thoughts, feelings and responses to what you just read.

_____

_____

_____

_____

_____

_____

_____

_____

_____

_____

_____

_____

_____

_____

_____

_____

_____

_____

I Have, She Has...

"For you formed my innermost part; You knit me [together] in my mother's womb. I will give thanks and praise to you, for I am fearfully and wonderfully made; Wonderful. Are your works, And my soul knows it very well. - Psalms 139: 13-14

Look at her sitting over there, she seems to always have everything. She has the hair that I've always wanted. She has the dress that I asked for but couldn't get. She gets to go out on dates and my parents said I need to wait. She got picked and I didn't. The boys are always around her and not me. She's always getting A's and I'm barely making it. I can't believe she could get that and I couldn't.

How many times have we heard but she has it? How many times have we looked and become a little covetous and envious? And all adults say to us is: "Just be thankful for what you have?" Do they not get it?

Why can't I have what she has?

Prayer: Lord, help me understand that You made me different and unique for a reason. Help me learn how to thank You and be pleased with what I have. Lord, I bind the spirits of covetousness, envy, comparison, and greed. I lose gratefulness, thankfulness, and contentment. Allow me to be thankful for all that You have given me and all that You have shielded me from by not allowing me to have what could have harmed me.

Declare: I was born at the right time, in the right place, to the right people, for God's purpose and, because God is the source for all I am and all I have, I am thankful.

Take a moment to capture your thoughts, feelings and responses to what you just read.

_____

_____

_____

_____

_____

_____

_____

_____

_____

_____

_____

_____

_____

_____

_____

_____

_____

Decision Time

I go to church every Sunday. I read my Bible during the week. I pray in the morning. I pray sometimes during school and I pray before I go to bed. I believe in God and I know that He loves me. I know what I'm supposed to do. I know what I am taught to do. But I am still conflicted.

On Sundays and when I'm reading my word, it seems so clear to me. I feel like I am ready to go and be on fire for the Lord and I'm going to live what the word tells me to do. I'm going to go out and be a true disciple. I'm going to go out and live the way Christ lived. I'm going to do better.

Then I leave the church, my house, my room and something happens. People really try me. Life starts life-ing. Before I know it I'm saying stuff, I'm doing stuff, I'm thinking stuff that is contrary to what the word says. I'm cursing, or I'm popping off at the mouth, or I'm talking about somebody, or I am giving attitude, or instigating, or I'm lying, or stealing, or smoking, or vaping, or I'm engaging in sexual activities, or I'm fighting, or being disobedient, or just rude and nasty. It just happens so fast.

I really want to do what the word says. I really want to please God. Why is it so hard? Why do I slip back so easily?

Prayer: Lord, help me make the right choices. Reveal to me what I need to remove from my life so that I can stay consistent in my walk of faith. Teach me how to live a life pleasing to You at all times. Teach me how to control my emotions, how to shut my mouth, how to stop being anxious, and how to stop moving before You direct me to do so. Let me learn how to truly crucify my flesh and choose You at all times.

Take a moment to capture your
thoughts, feelings and responses to
what you just read.

_____

_____

_____

_____

_____

_____

_____

_____

_____

_____

_____

_____

_____

_____

_____

I Just Want To Be Loved

"Love suffers long and is kind; love does not envy; love does not parade itself, is not puffed up; does not behave rudely, does not seek its own, is not provoked, thinks no evil; does not rejoice in iniquity, but rejoices in the truth; bears all things, believes all things, hopes all things, endures all things." - I Corinthians 13:4-7 NKJV

He says he loves me and I've never felt these feelings before. I see everybody with somebody. I just want to be like everyone else. People say we look cute together. He likes it when I spend all my time with him. We even go to sleep on the phone together. He wants to know my every move because he cares so much about me.

Girl Talk

We have issues like everyone else. At least I think it's like everyone else. When he gets mad, he yells and screams. He calls me names that really hurt and sometimes it is in front of other people, but it's my fault. I can do things to make people mad. I mean, my parents get mad at me and yell and scream so why wouldn't he? It's normal, right? He's just showing me he loves me.

He loves me so much, he wants to show me. Not only does he tell me but he wants to show me physically. He wants me to skip classes and go in corners so that I can show him how much I care about him. I don't want him to leave me and go to some other girl. He wants me to sneak out the house to meet him in places that I'm not supposed to go. He wants me to lie to my parents and tell them I'm going one place but really,

I am going to be with him. But all the girls are doing it, at least that's what they say. I just want him to love me so why not? Isn't that how you show a person you love them?

Sometimes if I make him really mad, he may push me. He may grab me and pull me back towards him when I'm trying to walk away because I'm upset. That's okay because he has never hit me. He's just showing his passion and his love for me and I really know that I want to be loved. When he plays around with me, he gets a little rough sometimes (punching my arm, pulling my hair, pushing me into the lockers and other students) but he says he's just playing. It's okay, that's how he shows he loves me.

This must be love. Or is it?

Prayer: Lord I know in Your word. It says: "For God, so love the world that He gave his only begotten Son." I know that You say: "Love thy neighbor as thy self." I know that you say: "The greatest of these is love." So Lord, I pray You lead me to scriptures that will reveal what love looks like. Help me separate my emotions from the truth of Your Word. Strengthen me that I may love myself and accept nothing less than the love You describe in Your word. Give me boldness to not sell myself short. Teach me to be OK with choosing to love myself properly over having someone on my arm.

Take a moment to capture your
thoughts, feelings and responses to
what you just read.

_____

_____

_____

_____

_____

_____

_____

_____

_____

_____

_____

_____

_____

_____

_____

_____

_____

Get Real

So Much in My Head

Why doesn't anybody get it? I know that I am a teenager. I know that I am what they consider a child. They say that my life should be easy, but it doesn't feel that way. There's so much that I have to do.

I have my friends, my homework, and my extracurricular activities. I am worried about getting into college and worried if I'll become what I want to be. What if I don't even know if that's what I want?

So much I have to think about every day. There is a test tomorrow! Did she say that about me? Is she my friend? Is he my friend? Does he like me, I mean, does he really like me? Oh my goodness, it's just so much!

Did I do my laundry? Wash the dishes. Take out the trash? Is my room clean? Did I turn off that light? Did I remember to lock the door when I left? Oh no, I think I forgot to get that paper signed? I can't miss the bus!

Then at school, I have to make sure I don't look at her in the hall because she already has an attitude and tried to start something with me. I don't want to get in trouble, but people keep trying me! I know they pushed me on purpose! Why is she in my face? Why is he doing the most? Is it really that serious? Why is there always drama around me?

Get Real

Why is this teacher always on my back? I can't believe I have a test in every subject, every Friday. How can I possibly remember all this work? Can this teacher slow down? I'm not getting this!

Why do some kids make it seem so easy? Is it just me? They say, "I'm just a child." They say, "I have no "real" responsibilities." They say, "My life should be easy." Why doesn't it feel like it?

Prayer: Lord, You know what I go through on a day-to-day basis. God You know the weight of the burdens I carry. Lord, You said for me to cast all my cares on You. Teach me how to give them all to You so that I can have peace. Teach me how to be a wise steward over my mouth, my attitude, my thoughts, and my actions. I want to learn how not to be controlled by my emotions, but to be controlled by the Holy Spirit. Teach me how to prioritize. Show me the resources that I need to help me be successful without being overwhelmed. Lord, I want to honor You and in doing so I know I will walk in the purpose that You have for me with peace, joy, and love. My heart Lord is to please you. Let me be pleasing to you.

Take a moment to capture your
thoughts, feelings and responses to
what you just read.

_____

_____

_____

_____

_____

_____

_____

_____

_____

_____

_____

_____

_____

_____

_____

_____

It Can Wait, Or Can It?

"Don't procrastinate – there's no time to lose." – Proverbs 6:4

Sometimes I get to a place where I really want to start something but then something else grabs my attention. Before I know it the day is over.

Sometimes I really intend on finishing but then the phone rings, I get a notification, a friend sends me a funny reel and now I'm in the vortex of social media and I just can't stop scrolling. I promise myself that I'm going to finish what I started, or study for the test, or do the homework; but before I know it, it's due and it's not done

As this year progresses, the incomplete assignments, the low grades, the late homework, and the zeros keep piling up. I know I am disappointing my parents and myself. I intend to start, and when I start I intend to finish, but things pull me and drag me away and before I know it, it's the due day!

Prayer: Lord help me win this battle against procrastination. You said that I am already victorious in You so I must believe the battle is already won. Help me make the right choices. Let me choose wisely.

Help me understand that I never know what tomorrow may bring so let me take advantage of the time and the day that You give me. Help me put my responsibilities first. Help me to organize and prioritize knowing that You are God of decency and order. Lord, I pray that my lifestyle begins to line up with Your word and that I allow You to order my steps.

STOP

Take a moment to capture your
thoughts, feelings and responses to
what you just read.

_____

_____

_____

_____

_____

_____

_____

_____

_____

_____

_____

_____

_____

_____

_____

_____

_____

_____

About the Author

Patrice Brown is a native of Washington DC. She is a loving mother of five and has been teaching high school for over a decade. She has held roles as a mentor, national trainer, teacher, leader, and public speaker. Patrice is a praise and worship minister of dance and her heart's desire is to walk in her God given purpose. She enjoys her quiet moments alone as well as adventurous moments with her children. Patrice's heart is to love all like Jesus and her prayer is that you are able to see her heart in her writing.

www.ingramcontent.com/pod-product-compliance
Lightning Source LLC
Chambersburg PA
CBHW060637030426
42337CB00018B/3392